Copyright © 2019 by Vivid Vivienne
All rights reserved. No part of this publication may be reproduced, distributed, or transmitted in any form or by any means, including photocopying, recording, or other electronic or mechanical methods, without the prior written permission of the author, except in the case of brief quotations embodied in critical reviews and certain other noncommercial uses permitted by copyright law. For permission requests email vvcolorbooks@gmail.com

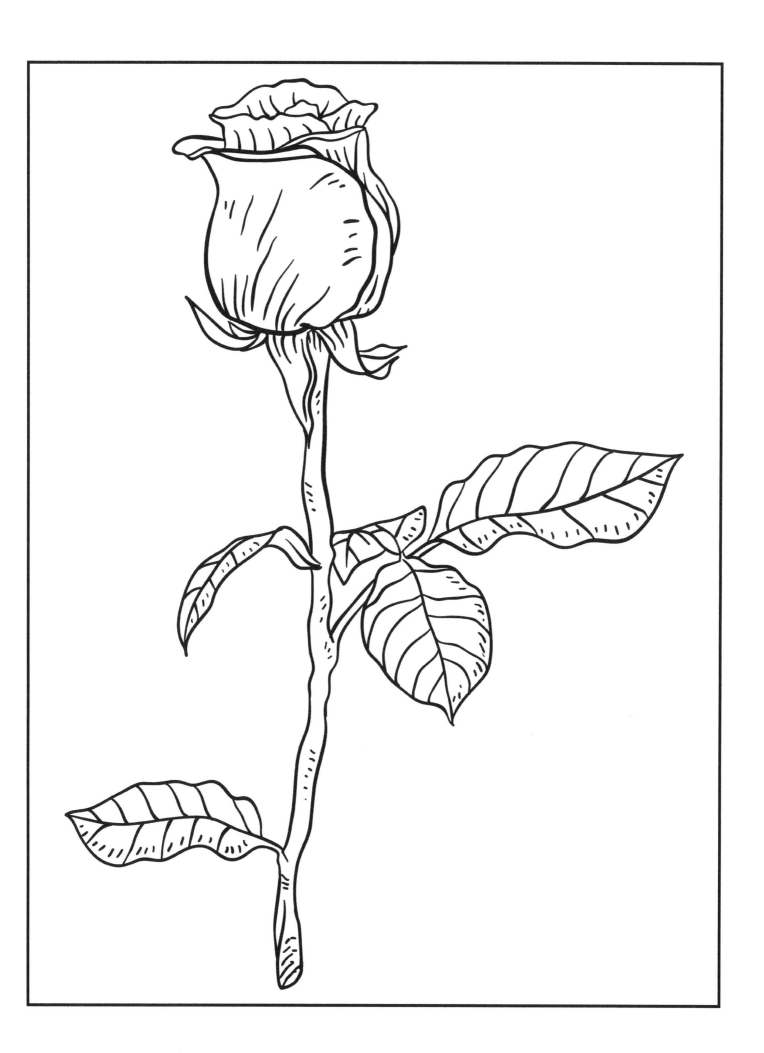

Enjoy this Book?

Be sure to check out Volume One

by Vivid Vivienne

Available now on Amazon!

FREE Bonus Flower PDF for you to print and color!

Simply email: VVcolorbooks@gmail.com

And Quote: Flower001

Thanks for Coloring!

CPSIA information can be obtained
at www.ICGtesting.com
Printed in the USA
BVHW010512080920
588278BV00017B/277